Law of Cause and Effect.

Law of Cause and Effect.

Series "Laws of the Universe "
By: Sherry Lee
Version 1.1 ~March 2023
Published by Sherry Lee at KDP
Copyright ©2023 by Sherry Lee. All rights reserved.

No part of this publication may be reproduced, distributed or transmitted in any form or by any means including photocopying, recording or other electronic or mechanical methods or by any information storage or retrieval system without the prior written permission of the publishers, except in the case of very brief quotations embodied in critical reviews and certain other noncommercial uses permitted by copyright law.

All rights reserved, including the right of reproduction in whole or in part in any form.

All information in this book has been carefully researched and checked for factual accuracy. However, the author and publisher make no warranty, express or implied, that the information contained herein is appropriate for every individual, situation, or purpose and assume no responsibility for errors or omissions.

The reader assumes the risk and full responsibility for all actions. The author will not be held responsible for any loss or damage, whether consequential, incidental, special, or otherwise, that may result from the information presented in this book.

All images are free for use or purchased from stock photo sites or royalty-free for commercial use. I have relied on my own observations as well as many different sources for this book, and I have done my best to check facts and give credit where it is due. In the event that any material is used without proper permission, please contact me so that the oversight can be corrected.

The information provided in this book is for informational purposes only and is not intended to be a source of advice or credit analysis with respect to the material presented. The information and/or documents contained in this book do not constitute legal or financial advice and should never be used without first consulting with a financial professional to determine what may be best for your individual needs.

The publisher and the author do not make any guarantee or other promise as to any results that may be obtained from using the content of this book. You should never make any investment decision without first consulting with your own financial advisor and conducting your own research and due diligence. To the maximum extent permitted by law, the publisher and the author disclaim any and all liability in the event any information, commentary, analysis, opinions, advice and/or recommendations contained in this book prove to be inaccurate, incomplete or unreliable, or result in any investment or other losses.

Content contained or made available through this book is not intended to and does not constitute legal advice or investment advice and no attorney-client relationship is formed. The publisher and the author are providing this book and its contents on an "as is" basis. Your use of the information in this book is at your own risk.

TABLE OF CONTENTS.

INTRODUCTION..3

CHAPTER 1: WHAT IS THE LAW OF CAUSE AND EFFECT?............5

CHAPTER 2: IS THE LAW OF CAUSE AND EFFECT IDENTICAL TO THE LAW OF ATTRACTION?..11

CHAPTER 3; HOW THE LAW OF CAUSE AND EFFECT AFFECTS YOUR PROFESSIONAL AND PERSONAL LIVES...............................13

CHAPTER 4; HOW TO IMPLEMENT THE LAW OF CAUSE AND EFFECT TO GET WHAT YOU WANT..23

CHAPTER 5; HOW THE LAW OF CAUSE AND EFFECT IS LINKED TO ACHIEVEMENT..26

CHAPTER 6; THE LAW OF CAUSE AND EFFECT OR KARMA..........28

CHAPTER 7: USE THE LAW OF CAUSE AND EFFECT TO MAKE MONEY..31

CHAPTER 8: LAW OF CAUSE AND EFFECT FOR SPIRITUAL DEVELOPMENT...33

CHAPTER 9; LEARN TO HAVE FAITH IN THE LAW OF CAUSE AND EFFECT..36

CHAPTER 10; HOW TO UTILIZE THE PSYCHOLOGICAL LAW OF CAUSE AND EFFECT FOR MASS PERSUASION WITH EASE............38

CHAPTER 11: HELPING OTHERS WITHOUT EXPECTING ANYTHING IN RETURN USING THE POWER OF CAUSE AND EFFECT..40

CHAPTER 12: THE LAW OF CAUSE AND EFFECT FOR CORPORATIONS..43

CHAPTER 13: HAVING BELIEF IN THE LAW OF CAUSE AND EFFECT 47

CHAPTER 14: LIVING THE LAW OF CAUSE AND EFFECT 51

CHAPTER 15: HOW TO SURVIVE UNDER A CHALLENGING SITUATION UTILIZING THE LAW OF CAUSE AND EFFECT............54

CHAPTER 16: CHOOSE A STRONG CAUSE TO APPLY THE LAW OF CAUSE AND EFFECT 57

CHAPTER 17: DON'T REMAIN CONFINED TO THE CHAINS OF CAUSE AND EFFECT 60

CONCLUSION 63

INTRODUCTION.

This book focuses on the Law of Cause and Effect. Based on the Socratic law of causation, this law is so profound and potent that it has been dubbed the "Iron Law of Human Fate." This is the third of seven Universal Laws in our ongoing series.

Constantly, we observe the universal rule of cause and effect at work in our environment. It asserts that accidents don't happen. For each outcome, there is a cause or collection of reasons. This is a universal law that has been observed for centuries. It asserts that there is a cause for all events. There is no such thing as random occurrences.

It is also crucial to note that this law is neither personal nor vindictive. Your power connection is severed if you fail to pay your electricity bills by the due date. Nothing personal is intended here. According to the rule of cause and effect, there is essentially no such thing as luck, coincidence, or chance in the world.

This applies not only to individual experiences but to the cosmos in general. If this were not true, the entire universe would have imploded instantly, and everything would have been in complete chaos.

Hence, you must pause and reflect on why life treats you unfairly. Have you given your 100 percent?

Why, then, do you anticipate the same?

How can you expect to pass your examinations if you did not prepare for them?

This should be interpreted as positive news. It is time to wake up if you contemplate leaving things to chance. You and you alone influence the outcomes of your life. Whether you or your life is joyful, unhappy, furious, unjust, satisfied, or unfulfilled, you are responsible for its current state. You are the director of the film known as life. You can be pleased with the outcome or weep over its inadequacies.

Nonetheless, it is essential to remember that life is what you make of it. Hence, it is not too late. Get up. Pass on. Pursue the realization of your dreams. You are the only thing keeping you back. Every day is significant. Every moment is an opening. Start living. Do what you find enjoyable.

As said previously, you reap what you sow. Even if every effect has a cause, that effect may not manifest immediately. In reality, a mixture of factors might result in an effect. You will only be able to feel the effects under specific conditions. And if you are not receiving what you desire in relationships, at work, with your family, or elsewhere, it is because you are not offering what you should.

It is your thoughts, habits, and actions that have manifested into the life you are currently living. If you are unhappy with this result, you must change its source. This implies that you must shift both your cognitive process and your mindset.

CHAPTER 1: WHAT IS THE LAW OF CAUSE AND EFFECT?

The Law of Cause and Effect is an astounding and significant natural law. This law can be expressed in two parts: first, everything has a cause and an effect; an effect can't exist without a cause, and a cause can't exist without an effect. Second, for every cause, there is an equal and opposite effect.

The universe is filled with energy, and everything is energy. This is the connection between us and the universe. This led to the conception of the law of cause and effect. Remember the ancient adage, "You receive what you give?" The law of attraction is similar to this adage.

Karma is a common term for describing the rule of cause and effect. According to the concept of karma, what you send out into the cosmos is what you will get back. You will attract negative circumstances if you are a negative person who constantly thinks, speaks, and acts poorly.

The cosmos will eventually return to you on its schedule. It is not true that the more positive ideas you have, the sooner they will return. Yet, positive things will return to you if you are positive.

Yeah, it is difficult to be optimistic with everything negative happening around you and affecting your life negatively. Yet, with a little practice, you might be among the 10% of those who genuinely understand how to implement the law of cause and effect to your advantage.

It is difficult always to stay optimistic while horrible things are happening, yet good things must happen. The cosmos will give you back what you give it.

For some advice on maintaining a happy outlook, you must first be able to "let go." You express your desires and aspirations and act as if you already own them, but then you let them go. Don't behave like a youngster by repeatedly requesting it.

If you are optimistic, your dream will come true when the timing is right. Make sure to read and converse with those who share your viewpoint. This will keep you motivated, as strength lies in numbers. If you exercise, you will obtain.

Nothing happens randomly; there is always an underlying cause. Anything that has happened or will happen is merely because of specific causes. Each cause is the consequence of a decision or action we made or did not make.

Our life is merely a reflection of all the causes and effects that we have chosen. If we desire different outcomes in life, we must change our actions. We can change these reasons by changing our ideas, emotions, and behaviors.

As you change your thinking, this changes your emotions, which changes your behaviors, which changes your outcomes. Hence, by changing just one item, your thoughts, you triggered a series of circumstances that led to very different outcomes.

The Law of Cause and Effect demonstrates that when we take action in the direction of our desires, our desires move in our direction. Every action always has an equal and opposite reaction. Every time you step away from yourself, a response returns in your direction.

This is an essential aspect of the law, implying that we only need to do fifty percent of the labor to achieve our objectives. To comprehend this, consider a boomerang. You launch the boomerang into the air, and it returns to you, or you push against a weight machine, and it pushes back, assisting you in achieving your goal of a stronger physique.

Any repressed negativity about someone returns to you multiplied. It may not manifest immediately, but it will manifest eventually. When individuals hold back too much negativity about others, it can manifest as fearful diseases such as migraines, Tuberculosis, and Cancer. Your life is too short to harbor resentment, anger, or vengeance against anyone.

Also, when you hold a grudge against someone, you can't feel good, and, as a result, you begin to attract all the undesirable experiences into your life. You will live in peace, happiness, and prosperity if you don't harbor grudges and ill will toward others.

Today, let's examine our own lives. If you observe, you won't notice that any company whose mission is to increase people's wealth, productivity, and connectivity is always a huge success.

Consider, for instance, the telecommunications, power, retail, software, and networking industries; all these industries are expanding at a breakneck pace. Because these firms boost people's productivity, connectedness, and standard of living, they contribute to their growth.

Companies must be structured to help others become prosperous first. According to the Law, the more you help others grow, the more you will likewise flourish.

When you begin constructing enterprises and cultures intentionally meant to give rather than receive, you will achieve even greater success.

Usually, greed, anger, deceit, and dishonesty are the root causes of evil. Conflict and imbalance ensue when the basis is not based on genuine mutual benefit. If you are generating abnormally high profits at the expense of your company partners, you will eventually cause yourself harm. Thus, it violates the Law of Cause and Effect.

Let's look at another illustration: it is common knowledge that every country's government spends massive amounts of money on its defense. Every day, billions of dollars are spent on the world's armies, navies, and air forces. Yet, all these costs would have been completely unnecessary without global peace.

The money spent on the army, navy, and air force is, in general, a complete waste. If peace existed everywhere, this enormous amount of money could be spent on other economically beneficial and uplifting pursuits. It would have made the world a vastly superior place to live.

The funds could have provided the poor and needy with equal opportunities. This would have enabled them to establish companies and support themselves. It would have been a much better, more peaceful, and prosperous world.

To clarify the law of Cause and Effect, you must first give to receive in life. The purpose of life is to create the highest quality of giving, not the highest quality of receiving. You should only be concerned about what you will give.

We keep forgetting this, but life is not about receiving but about giving! And to do so, you must be able to forgive others, particularly those who did not deliver what you expected.

The law of Cause and Effect is, however, only one facet of The Big Eternal Law, which I have written below. There is an alternative perspective on The Law of Cause and Effect.

Permit me to ask:

What motivates people to take action in their lives?

Why was I motivated to compose this book?

Why are individuals motivated to begin a career, business, passion, or hobby?

They seek to initiate that something, but something else is happening in the background, behind the scenes.

This motivation is caused by the collective consciousness of all the individuals in the world. The universe has also played a significant role in your inspiration. Therefore, the reason you have an idea is partially due to the actions of others. This is also known as the "invisible law of supply and demand."

When a sufficient number of people start desiring and believing they can have a particular type of car (for example), the universe will cause a person with the appropriate level of desire and belief to enter the automobile industry, create that car and sell it to the people who generated the demand.

The reason you have an idea is in part due to the actions of others. The next time you get inspiration, an inner sensation, or a nudge, rejoice in the knowledge that a group of individuals (no matter how little or vast) is actively urging you to achieve their desires. In this manner, the cosmos satisfy all of our desires and beliefs.

This is how the universe serves as a mediator to help people assist others in achieving their goals. You are the solution to their prayers and desires, and they are the solution to yours. This brings us back to the principle of attraction; thus, our lives come full circle. It is sometimes referred to as the circle of life.

I will provide an example from my own life to illustrate this law.

In high school, an individual prepared for the two-mile race. As the season began, I hadn't been training and therefore had the same skill, or lack thereof, as anyone else in my situation. I began competitive preparations by running eight or more miles every day. Initially, I ran two miles, then four, until I averaged ten miles daily. At this training level, I could compete with the other runners in the race.

How did I go from running a slow mile to a quick ten-mile? The solution can be found in the law of cause and effect. Resistance developed as I drove my muscles to run faster and for longer durations, strengthening my legs and body.

In addition, as I put force away from myself into the earth to propel myself forward, a response happened that assisted me. The reaction was the ground's equal resistance to my force, allowing me to continue. Without both of these occurrences, I would not have been able to develop my running abilities.

Remember that everything has a cause and effect. Discover the reason for the desired outcomes, and your life will flourish.

CHAPTER 2: IS THE LAW OF CAUSE AND EFFECT IDENTICAL TO THE LAW OF ATTRACTION?

The Law of Attraction and the Law of Cause and Effect differ. The latter is derived from the former. In other words, the universe is perfectly balanced due to the Law of Cause and Effect. Cause and effect must be similar to Newton's Third Law.

Due to this ideal equilibrium, we have the Law of Attraction. That is not a case of chicken and egg. They would have developed contemporaneously. The concept of Cause and Effect led science for millennia until a group of Greek scientists introduced the theory of Chance-Events and muddied the waters.

This, however, should not be confused with the Chaos Theory. In 1960, a meteorologist was the first to promote this concept, which is wholly distinct. If a butterfly flaps its wings in a certain way in the Brazilian rainforest, would this trigger a tornado in Peoria or elsewhere? This is now a distinct branch of research.

In the nineteenth century, the Chance-Events theory took root as the Heisenberg Uncertainty Principle, and its influence grew in the twentieth. The arguments for and against the Heisenberg Principle were vast and heated, but it has since been discredited on six grounds, which we won't discuss here.

There is no doubt that Cause and Effect, along with the Law of Attraction, Vibration, and Development, rule the universe, and now we reach the most essential aspect of the Law of Attraction. Vibration.

Every object vibrates. We can't necessarily see the vibration, but it exists nonetheless. You will observe movement when you place a leaf fragment under a strong microscope. Neither can you see nor feel the vibration just by observing the leaf, but it is present.

A dog whistle is an excellent example. The sound is inaudible to us, but all the neighborhood dogs will be barking their heads off!

As we have seen, the Universe is in perfect equilibrium. If this weren't the case, we would all be propelled into outer space, suns and planets would collide everywhere, and there would be absolute anarchy.

We may discover a mystery after we die, but I don't believe it has anything to do with theology. For the Universe to be perfectly balanced, there must be an Intelligence that our puny minds can't even begin to comprehend. Are you God? If you like.

This Intelligence is fundamentally identical to our own in that it vibrates and consists of pure energy, similar to ours in this regard. However, please don't misread this statement. I am in no way attempting to place us on an equal footing.

Before considering the Law of Attraction, you must accept responsibility for your past actions. Why are you still struggling like most of us? It's because you've made decisions that have proven to be unwise.

Your riches must originate from within as a "wealth consciousness." Nevertheless, you must first discover who you truly are. You are not who you were raised to believe you were. Forget all of that and pursue your true self.

CHAPTER 3; HOW THE LAW OF CAUSE AND EFFECT AFFECTS YOUR PROFESSIONAL AND PERSONAL LIVES.

When starting a business, it is crucial to have a well-thought-out plan that has been thoroughly researched, written, studied, analyzed, and refined before execution to ensure a good start and minimize mistakes along the way. According to the proverb, "If you fail to plan, you plan to fail."

It is your advantage to create the business plan yourself, regardless of how "rough" it may appear to an experienced business writer. Request professional assistance but don't let anyone else write your business plan.

You are not writing for the Wall Street Journal; rather, you are composing your success formula. A business writer may not share your passion for your "baby," which is the foundation of your success formula. A good business plan is not assessed by how well its success-feasibility writes but by its.

Even for a "simple" home-based business, the significance of a business plan can't be overstated, and avoid letting your business plan collect dust on a bookshelf. Make it your quick-access reference material by dog-earing its pages. Always revise your work to keep up with evolving technologies and fashions.

But there is something even more important than the business plan that you must consider early on — and always remember — if you are truly dead serious in your pursuit of success, whether with your planned business or the much larger business of living your LIFE, which was intended for you to enjoy when you were brought into this green sphere we call earth. The Almighty Creator, who filled the globe with plenty, did not intend for man to live in unhappiness despite the abundance.

First, you must accept that there is no such thing as blind chance, accident, or luck in the natural world. Everything (tangible or intangible, physical or spiritual) is governed by specific and active Universal Rules established by the Great Lawgiver.

You can disagree, but your disagreement doesn't invalidate the existence of such laws. Consider, for instance, the Law of Gravity. If this law did not exist, do you believe anything would exist on Earth, say at the equator, where the planet revolves 1,038 miles per hour?

What would happen if the earth abruptly ceased to rotate?

This chapter does not intend to educate you on all the Universal Laws; there are simply too many to mention here (space would not permit it even if I wanted to). However, there is one particular law that I would like to share with you: the Law of Cause and Effect and the related law, the Law of Financial Success.

For every Effect, there is a Cause; for every Cause, there is an Effect.

Here's how one astute writer phrased it:

"Given identical circumstances, a given Cause will always have the same effect. This is what is known as "Law." If we could do a detailed investigation of our lives, we would discover that they are the consequence or product of the Law. Without a "Cause," a "Effect" is impossible. Hence if we want to control the effect, we must first activate the proper Cause.

"We are so accustomed to accepting thoughts, methods, and conditions which have been handed down from our ancestors or which are the result of social or economic evolution, as the only right thing and binding upon us and to attributing the various things that come to us to "Chance," that we can't initially comprehend the magnitude of the fact that in our entire Life-expression, we are governed and controlled absolutely by Law!

It initially astounds us, and while we can discern the workings of Laws in certain spheres, we are slow to grasp the transcendent truth that in everything that concerns us, including our Success or Failure, Plenty or Poverty, Happiness or Unhappiness and Health or Disease, ALL is governed and determined by Law!"

The Law goes into effect the instant you allow a concept to enter your mind (Cause), reflect on it, and act upon it. As you determine things in your mind, they shape and materialize appropriately (Effect).

When unleashed, the mind's inherent power may transform landscapes and remake civilizations. The Almighty Creator Himself acknowledges the power of the intellect to produce a proportional Cause and Effect. As He halted mankind's desire to build the Tower of Babel to dizzying heights, He declared, "Now that they have begun to do this, they will be able to accomplish EVERYTHING they set out to do."

Implementing the Legislation.

Consider for a moment why you intend to establish your firm. What is your purpose, motivation, or objective? What is your vision? Your dream?

Well, yes. VISION. How many of the world's 6 billion inhabitants have a vision?

The Book of Proverbs states, "Where there is no vision, the people die; but blessed is he who keeps the law." Have you observed this book's correlation between vision and the law?

Money is not the ultimate goal of life. If your primary motivation for starting a business is to generate tons of money, you should reconsider. Because there is so much to say about money, there is insufficient room for a more extensive discussion in this chapter. Still, the King Midas story (you must be familiar with it) that I've given below will put everything into perspective:

King Midas.

King Midas was a compassionate guy who ruled his kingdom justly but never gave any thought to what he said. While strolling around his yard one day, he saw an ancient satyr dozing among the flowers.

Having compassion for the elderly man, King Midas released him without punishment. When the deity Dionysus learned of this, he rewarded King Midas with one desire. The monarch pondered momentarily, declaring, "I wish everything I touch would become gold." Thus it was.

The beautiful flowers in his garden leaned toward the sun for illumination, but when Midas touched them, they became hard and solid gold. Each time the king attempted to eat, he discovered that his food had been transformed into gold. Under his loving touch, his beautiful daughter turned into solid gold. His water, his bed, his clothes, his friends, and ultimately, his entire palace were all made of gold.

King Midas saw that his entire realm would turn to gold if he did not act immediately. He requested that

Dionysus restore everything to its original state and retrieve his golden touch. Because of the king's disgrace and extreme sadness, Dionysus had compassion for him and granted his request. Immediately, King Midas was poorer than he had been but felt richer in what mattered.

The Financial Success Law.

Return to your intended activities. The brief story of King Midas demonstrates how the mind processes and how the Law of Cause and Effect applies to thought.

No one could deny that making money is the primary goal of a business because why would someone start a business if he did not intend for it to be profitable?

Money can be perceived in two ways:

- Money is a means to an end.

- Money is an end in itself.

One author characterizes the two techniques as follows:

"According to this perspective (money as an end), money should be pursued. That is the ultimate purpose of the endeavor. This strategy allows for the accumulation and immobilization of funds, and immobilization implies unequal distribution, which means that money will accrue more heavily for some (the wealthy) and be rare and scant for others (the poor).

This is the case since there is a limited supply of money under this strategy. Consequently, the ultimate goal should be to amass as much wealth as possible, which provides "stability" and "financial freedom."

"In (approaching money as a means), the notion is that money is a means to the final goal of experiencing something, solely for the joy and pleasure accompanying the event. Money is not the end goal; it is the things money may purchase. Money is only a medium of exchange for purchasing or selling products and/or services that can fulfill desires. In this system, money doesn't accumulate but rather circulates.

How do you personally feel about money?

Do you view it as a "goal" or a "means to an end"?

Now, you apply this perspective to your planned business. Everything must be crystal clear from the outset. Thus, your decisions will focus on what is right rather than practical.

Would you get into business to accumulate a fortune? Do you "sense" the urge to save money in the bank for "security" and "independence"?

During the Great Depression, there was a story about a retired old man who, upon scanning the day's newspaper one morning, discovered that all the money he had in the bank — his entire life's savings — was worth only one round-trip ticket around Berlin. You are aware of what he did, correct?

He withdrew all his funds, purchased a ticket, toured Berlin, returned home, closed the door, and shot himself to death.

Don't pursue wealth as if it were the only thing that counts. Want instead the things money can buy that will improve your quality of life. Someone once observed, "Money is a poor master and a loyal servant." Indeed. According to the Great Master, "what does it profit a man to obtain the entire world but lose his soul?"

Do you have a viable business concept?

Go for it but don't become a slave to the money. The only way to acquire substantial wealth is to put money to work for you." according to one author, "no man has ever become extremely wealthy by working with his hands alone; the same is true for brain workers."

That's all there is to it. Use the money to your advantage. Make your money grow by investing it wisely. The purpose of money is circulation, not hoarding. I am not suggesting that you should not save. You should prepare for "rainy days." Don't be stingy and greedy at the same time is the point I'm trying to make.

Learn from Nature, as it is never self-centered. It adequately provides for all of man's necessities, not just for survival but also for enjoyment. Air, water, sunlight, and the plants and animals that give you food, clothes, and shelter are replenished every morning, providing you with everything you require for survival.

Have you ever observed that the grass you mowed the day before produced new blades to greet the morning sun?

Your pruning hurt those annoying weeds, yet it did not prevent them from carrying out Nature's design. They did not contract but instead produced new leaves.

Does it upset you that the flowers you chose from your garden withered in the evening? No, since you knew you would have enough supply of replacements the following day. When you pruned your fruit trees, did you worry they would no longer produce fruit? No, because you were aware that by removing the branches, the trees would regenerate new ones and produce even more fruit.

Hence, this is how you should manage your finances. Use thrift but don't hoard, and while your chest fills with pride, accomplish something even more valuable, such as making a difference in a world gone insane.

Bill Gates, the richest man in the world, is no longer involved in the daily operations of Microsoft, the firm he fought tooth and nail to establish as the largest software empire in the world. He continues to have an impact on people's lives. Through the Bill & Melinda Gates Foundation, he actively spearheads the fight against malaria while enjoying life.

Early on, he had a crystal-clear picture of his Goal, which he pursued with tenacious determination and against all difficulties. He had confidence in his abilities. He had a Purpose: "Windows® in every desktop." He made significant contributions to productivity, growth, and the never-ending advancement of technology. He was effective in his conduct. Many refer to him as "filthy rich" due to his success.

Do you believe he followed certain laws and principles to become the extremely wealthy man he is today? You bet he did. Money did not miraculously fall into his lap. Nor did he sit all day yearning for money to fall from the sky or flow into his bank account from the vaults of Swiss banks.

Because he was in perfect accordance with the Universal Rules that govern financial prosperity, namely:

- The Cause and Effect Law (Opening the Way with a Workable Plan).
- The Action and Response Law (The more you give, the more you receive)
- The Law of Thankfulness (Be grateful even for the little things that come your way).
- The Attraction Law ("As A Man Thinketh In His Heart, So Is He").

And the underlying principles:

- Vision (Definiteness and fixedness of Purpose)
- Faith (Confidence in one's Capabilities)
- Effective Behavior ("Be The Best of Whatever You Are")
- Will and Resoluteness ("Never Surrender").
- Anticipation and Persistence (Only dead fish float downriver)
- A Positive Mental Attitude (Build your ideals and live in them mentally)

The accumulation of money is governed by the Law of Financial Success, comprised of the abovementioned rules and principles. To get wealthy, one must follow a "Specific Method," similar to following mathematical formulas when solving math problems. It is impossible to arrive at the result "1" while using the formula "1 + 1."

If some smooth-talking "guru" tells you that to become wealthy, all you need to do is follow the Law of Attraction as depicted in "The Secret," don't believe them. The law in question is only one of the variables that influence success.

No amount of longing, wishing, envisioning, or visualizing for your planned business would enable you to achieve your goals if you spend all day in bed or dream your life away in Peter Pan-style Never Never Land.

I am not naive enough to tell you that this chapter is all you need to have a successful home-based business. I urge you to learn all you can about entrepreneurship and fully equip yourself with the skills necessary to accomplish your dream.

I can only hope to teach you the correct knowledge and understanding of the fundamentals of a home-based company and the Universal Laws and Principles that "control and determine the outcome of our every action-the, the success or failure of every endeavor!"

If, at this stage, you have a complete mental picture of your intended business, don't hesitate for a second. ACT NOW. Time doesn't wait for anyone.

Wipe from your mind any thoughts leading you to doubt your ability and capability to carry out your plan until you can envision yourself on vacation in the Bahamas, unconcerned about your business as it continues to generate money for you around the clock on autopilot.

If you follow the Law of Financial Success outlined in this chapter and do what is expected of you, especially in the early stages of your home-based business, things should go well for you and your enterprise. Simply do it.

"YES, YOU CAN." Obama utilized eloquent language to inspire and motivate crowds to elect him to the most powerful position on the planet. You can also say "YES, I CAN" to yourself.

CHAPTER 4; HOW TO IMPLEMENT THE LAW OF CAUSE AND EFFECT TO GET WHAT YOU WANT.

Based on the Law of Cause and Effect, everything happens for a reason. Whether conscious or unconscious, our decisions are causes that produce matching consequences or effects. All acts and inactions have consequences and yield unique outcomes. The law applies uniformly to everyone at all times.

This law states that for every outcome or effect in a person's life, there is a specific cause: poor diet and exercise habits result in poor health, constant and uncontrolled spending results in debt and money worries, and not putting effort into your key relationships results in poor relationships and all the associated problems.

Examining Sir Isaac Newton's Third Law of Motion, which asserts "for every action, there is an equal and opposite reaction," enables the actual application of the law. If, for instance, you held your hand over the flame of a candle (the cause), the impact would be that your hand would burn and hurt! Although this is an extreme example, it effectively illustrates the point.

Consider another enterprise-specific circumstance. Imagine if your company is so successful that it can't keep up with demand - a pleasant problem! While your personnel strives to address the issue, the quality of customer care deteriorates over time. Complaints are received, and employee morale begins to decline.

You can now attempt to make do with the current situation or hire other personnel. This is a challenging decision since many unknowns are associated with recruiting - will you find the perfect person, will he or she be part of the solution or the problem, what will happen to your cash flow, etc.?

Any decision you make - to hire or not to hire - becomes the cause. The effect is the consequence of the choice. If you recruited someone, your current employees should feel relieved, and your customers should be happier with your service (providing, of course, you hired the right person and invested in training them properly).

If the decision to not hire was made, the result would likely be unsatisfied customers and possibly lost staff unless another solution (cause) could be identified (process re-engineering, etc.). This is a recipe for disaster that might easily result in the total failure of the business.

The same applies to your interpersonal interactions. Suppose you treat the key people in your life with respect, love, compassion, dignity, and honesty (cause). In that case, you will have loving, enduring relationships, leading to happiness, fulfillment, and peace of mind (effect).

Making It Benefit You:

The great aspect of this law is that, by definition, we should be able to materialize what we truly desire (the outcome) by exerting the same causes that others have exerted before us with success. Let me explain:

If you want to be a highly paid and successful businessperson in your chosen industry, you should look back and analyze what made others successful. What books did they read, what courses did they take, what views did they have, and what acts did they perform?

If you were to imitate what they did to attain success, you would obtain the same outcomes over time. If this doesn't happen over time, it is likely due to a change in what you were doing or the absence of an essential piece of information.

What You Should Do:

There are three instant action exercises you can implement to assist you in achieving more of what you want:

1. Identify the Cause and Effect links in the areas where improvement or success is desired. Determine the particular actions you must take to get the desired results.

2. Take decisive action! Decide to focus on and implement other successful individuals' strategies in these fields. The other half of the battle is action. Your skill to initiate will differentiate you from the bulk of the populace.

3. Persevere. If you take action and do what others have done, you will eventually achieve your objectives. Remain focused, assess your causes to verify you are doing the right things, and adjust your strategy as needed - you will get the intended outcomes! Don't quit if it doesn't work immediately; success takes time. Rome wasn't built in a day, and reaching your current position has taken you a lifetime.

There is no secret to success; we all have access to it. Only awareness, comprehension, and living following Universal Law are required!

CHAPTER 5; HOW THE LAW OF CAUSE AND EFFECT IS LINKED TO ACHIEVEMENT.

Causality. You can have heard this word or someone else use it before but have you ever pondered its meaning? What is its impact on you? Moreover, how does it impact your success?

The term causality is derived from cause and effect. It means that for every action you take, there will be a corresponding reaction or consequence, but will the ensuing response or effect be just what you hoped for and desired?

Or will the response be something you detest and had no desire to attain in the first place?

For instance, if you ate a wonderful buffet with various exotic and mouth-watering delicacies and experienced stomach problems, did you want it to happen, or were you simply trying to fill your empty stomach?

Success doesn't happen by accident. It is highly dependent on the focused decisions and decisions you make and your effective actions (cause). In reality, success closely resembles the rule of cause and effect.

Then and only then would it be feasible to observe the expected beneficial results and outcomes (effect).

This can be proven by a simple comparison involving a student who determines and concentrates on achieving exceptional grades on his examination and studies diligently and intelligently. Eventually, he earns exceptional grades and eventually finishes first in his class.

Internet marketing is yet another highly important illustration of the correlation between causality and success. A simplistic example: a web marketer may have the ambition and concentration to become wealthy.

Afterward, he takes measures to attract visitors to his website, entice buyers with a persuasive sales letter, and provide exclusive products and substantial content. This will produce substantial sales and earnings for his website and himself.

The testing and tracking of variables such as unique visitors, conversion rates, subscriptions, direct sales, affiliate sales, etc., clearly demonstrate the applicability of the law of cause and effect in internet marketing - or any other industry for that matter.

Hence, the next time you hear or think about causality, do yourself a favor and ask yourself the following:

1) What choices and decisions do I wish to make?

2) What particular and efficient steps should I take?

3) How will these choices, decisions, and actions influence my success?

4) Were my earlier outcomes and successes mere accidents? Or were they direct repercussions of the actions I took?

There is no doubt that you will attain greater levels of success if you consistently keep the law of cause and effect in mind.

CHAPTER 6; THE LAW OF CAUSE AND EFFECT OR KARMA.

Many individuals worldwide believe in reincarnation and karma, although this belief is religiously divisive. In metaphysical and philosophical communities of thought, karma is often discussed. Sometimes you can discover gold in the comments, but using the term karma often misses the concept's essence.

Karma is a Sanskrit word, but it is being defined worldwide by individuals (including myself) who don't speak Sanskrit as their native tongue; as a result, we may or may not comprehend the phrase accurately. The only Sanskrit word we know or apply is karma. In my view, karma is widely misunderstood in metaphysical and philosophical circles and in general.

I begin with the word's origin to comprehend its usage and application. I have six-foot-tall, thirty-inch-wide bookcases containing my collection of eastern philosophy books, many of which I have read, so I am not without resources. Yet, I am not a practitioner of eastern philosophy. Along with most metaphysical or philosophic types, eastern principles have permeated my study.

I am continually fascinated by the philosophies of many cultures and their usually unconscious influence on my life. I need to understand the words and thoughts they denote, regardless of their origins. This series serves as an introduction to metaphysics; hence, simplicity is preferable at this point of comprehension.

According to the eMac dictionary, the source of the Sanskrit term karman denotes action, result, and destiny. Simply expressed, karma is an eastern philosophical idea corresponding to the law of cause and effect in our western civilization.

In a lifetime, we make tens of millions of decisions that result in behaviors, resulting in natural reactions, outcomes, or repercussions. Whether these activities are conscious or unconscious makes no difference.

We put them in motion through our actions or inactions, and we can be certain that there will be consequences. In my opinion, as part of our daily lives, most of these decisions or actions are initiated and experienced unconsciously. We typically don't consider our decisions and activities to be cause-and-effect at the time they are initiated. Still, we will eventually reap the natural effects of those decisions and acts.

Occasionally, these consequences are unique and particular, resulting from a single cause. Occasionally, these impacts can be collective, making it more difficult to identify or explain a single origin for a simple example.

Depending on how busy I am when I wake up, I may or may not eat breakfast. Consuming breakfast can fuel my physical vehicle (my body), and I will be prepared to face the world. I may be unable to face the world after consuming the same meal due to digestive distress; I may have to stay home to deal with this distress.

Because I am on a diet, I might skip breakfast and wish I had or congratulate myself on my iron will. That would make my day better. Perhaps the lack of food will cause me to become dizzy, disoriented, or irritable.

Possibly, I will get beyond dizzy and faint from lack of food. I could land safely or strike my skull or another bodily part on the way down (gravity will win in this instance). Hopefully, I won't encounter this in traffic or under hazardous conditions. Whether I choose to eat or not to eat is the causal factor; everything else is a result.

Whether you say yes to an experience no, throw your hands up and refuse to participate, or declare it is none of your business or responsibility, results will happen that is ours since we set them in action.

These outcomes may be known or unknown to us, yet we own them regardless of our ignorance. Why?

Because effect follows logically from causation, Consider the countless options that exist daily—the various causes.

You should be able to see that it is prudent to make every possibility on the causal end as favorable as possible because you will be responsible for the effects on the other end. These are, in a sense, the ingredients that eventually lead to karma.

The karma that metaphysicists typically speak to suggests a much broader impact, but this is the simplest explanation I could come up with to illustrate the origins of karma.

CHAPTER 7: USE THE LAW OF CAUSE AND EFFECT TO MAKE MONEY.

Many individuals understand and use the Law of Cause and Effect. Many others view this potent law just in terms of its spirituality and never bother to investigate its implications. This chapter describes how to utilize this legislation to become wealthy.

Agreeing with the Law of Cause and Effect, also known as the Law of Sowing and Reaping, acknowledges that "nothing happens for nothing" and "there is no smoke without fire." To acknowledge that there was a cause for every effect, and for every harvest, there was sowing. In other words, in Nature, there are no accidents, only consequences.

Hence, if you are poor, there are reasons, and if you are wealthy, there are also reasons. Nothing, nothing at all, happens without a CAUSE, and we are liable, whether via omission or commission.

As there is a causal force behind every result, condition, or experience, all that is required to change a result is to change its underlying cause. Hence, you must engage in activities that generate wealth to become wealthy. Stop engaging in activities that lead to poverty if you don't wish to remain poor.

When you stop doing the things that keep the poor poor and begin doing the things that make the rich affluent, there is no reason why you won't become wealthy.

In other words, your financial situation is predictable in life. That is deliberate, not accidental. It depends on your knowledge and activities; it is the result you make through your actions.

If you attempt diligently to become wealthy but are not, you should consider why. Look within; be sincere with yourself! Do you possess the mental attitude necessary for success?

Do you hold the correct beliefs about money? Invest your time and effort in pursuits that will bring you the wealth you seek.

Possibly your current job, business, or career is not leading you to the desired level of life. Why then adhere to it? Make a change! Do whatever it takes to set in action the necessary causal forces to generate the desired results.

If you sincerely desire riches, you must also be ready to do whatever it takes to obtain them. If you want an effect, you must call upon its causal factors! The farmer must seed before he can harvest and harvests what he sows: potato for potato and wheat for wheat.

Want to be wealthy?

Do you have a plan of action?

Are you executing the strategy?

What financial seeds are you planting now, and what financial harvest do you anticipate tomorrow?

Recall that every seed produces according to its species.

Everything you receive from life is proportional to what you put into it. Our decisions and actions are the chisels we carve out our earthly destinies. Indeed, every result has a corresponding cause.

CHAPTER 8: LAW OF CAUSE AND EFFECT FOR SPIRITUAL DEVELOPMENT.

It is commonly stated that every action has an equal and opposite reaction. More often than not, the intensity of your thoughts and emotions determines your disposition or, more specifically, the state of your energy and its vibration.

What is happening or not happening around you directly mirrors your present vibrational state.

Have you ever observed that things that ordinarily annoy you simply pass you by when you are in a good mood?

Have you also observed that the number of unpleasant situations and nasty individuals around you increases when your energy is low due to a disagreement with a loved one?

This is the Universal Law of Causal Relationships. There is a reaction to every action. If you are feeling sorry for yourself or focusing solely on the absence of anything in your life, you will attract more of the same. More lack, more negativity, more inappropriate companions.

Respecting where you are while maintaining your attention on what and where you want to go is, according to my understanding of Universal Laws, distinct from lingering in denial, confusion, or allowing your energy to remain in a bad vibration for an extended period.

Do you recall hearing, "you will harvest what you sow?" If yes, what does this mean?

That means that if you tend to your inner-Self, your Spirit, with negative self-talk and believe and own what people say about you, you will only cultivate the seeds of doubt, confusion, disappointment, betrayal, and financial hardship.

When you become more aware of who you truly are, your conscious awareness grows and expands, allowing you to be aware of and process your emotions much more swiftly. It allows you to eliminate energy blocks, bringing more of what you truly desire into your life.

If you are willing to examine yourself, release what no longer serves you, and initiate or continue the healing process, your energy will transform. When you change your energy, you will gain greater clarity on the path ahead, the people in your life, and how you radiate and project your light.

You will also realize that people and circumstances are leaving your life to make room for more of what you want.

Most people dislike the term "change." I will be the first to say that I dislike technological change. Changes must be made to attract more positive chances, relationships, and clients into your experience and daily life.

Regarding upgrades, I no longer kick and scream but still take many deep breaths and occasionally roll my eyes. If there are more than two buttons or options, I must concentrate on overcoming my spiritual resistance to change.

Technology is not always intuitive, requiring me to utilize my left brain, the analytical side of things. I greatly prefer to reside in the cozy right hemisphere of the brain.

Since they are woven into the very fabric of the universe, the Universal Laws are absolute. If you want things and your life, in particular, to be different, to attract your Soul Mate or Life Partner, but what you're doing isn't working, you should examine your activities.

What you send out into the cosmos is what you receive back. It is that straightforward. However, it is not always easy to accept that we are the architects of our lives.

Stay the same or choose to make a decision and take action to create new, more beneficial results merely by making positive energy shifts.

CHAPTER 9; LEARN TO HAVE FAITH IN THE LAW OF CAUSE AND EFFECT.

Every effect has a cause, and every cause has an effect. How can you distinguish between cause and effect?

Do you contribute to the production of either? If yes, what is your function? If you don't, is there someone or something that plays a function for you in this rule of cause and effect?

These inquiries directly penetrate the core of everything and every environmental condition, including ourselves. The following is the rule of thumb I've learned and used to distinguish between cause and effect. Effect encompasses everything observable to the physical senses, i.e., sight, hearing, taste, touch, and smell. Anything not apparent to the physical senses resides in the world of causes.

I believe that all causes exist within you, just as all causes about me exist within me. Consciousness comprises my thoughts, ideas, beliefs, and mental representations. Cause consists of the never-ending string of possibilities presented to me in consciousness from which I choose.

I can anticipate the outcome by selecting from the options and making my selection the focus of my attention and observation (the cause). This is the catch. If I don't consciously choose from the unending stream of alternatives, I nevertheless create choices (causes) unwittingly and unconsciously.

By failing to deliberately select the thoughts, ideas, and mental images on which to concentrate, my past experiences determine the focus of my attention. When the result of that unintentional, unconscious choice (cause) manifests in my experience (effect), I will likely attribute it to other effects.

Be cautioned. Occasional, lackadaisical focus can't be considered a cause and is unlikely to impact your life outcomes significantly. A pound of salt added to Lake Michigan won't transform it into a saltwater lake. However, sending a strong stream of salt into the lake over an extended period will significantly change the lake's composition.

I am confident that you can now see, as I have, that mastering your mind power is essential to gaining access to more of life's riches. There are riches available to you. It is completely irrelevant what your life circumstances have been up until this time.

You can now shift your consciousness in the direction of your desires, or you can continue doing so. If you make your desires the object of your attention (the cause), you will no longer be required to live in fear and anxiety regarding the effects you experience.

Once you have accepted the object of your focus into your deeper mind (the cause), let the Law of Cause and Effect take effect. If permitted, it must deliver the desired result (effect). Don't search the effects around you for the manifestation of your desire.

Each time you examine the world of effects and don't find it, you will likely reinforce your old belief that YOU DON'T HAVE IT. In effect, you begin to resist your desire before it can manifest.

This I am certain of. You can assert or reassert control over your mind power. You are the most miraculous creature on the planet. You are the owner of a mind so spectacular that as soon as you genuinely begin managing and deliberately employing your mental power, there is no goal that you can't accomplish.

CHAPTER 10; HOW TO UTILIZE THE PSYCHOLOGICAL LAW OF CAUSE AND EFFECT FOR MASS PERSUASION WITH EASE.

The human brain is wired to perceive cause-and-effect links even when none exist. Evolutionary biologists believe that this is done to save mental effort. Studies have also demonstrated that newborns perceive causal linkages where none exist.

This might be utilized when persuading others.

How?

Use whatever they are doing or experiencing as the cause and generate a desire or interest in your desired end as the impact. If you can figure out a couple of various ways to express this basic phrase and thread them into an otherwise typical discussion, you'll be able to have considerable influence.

They can also be chained. A causes B, which produces C, which in turn creates D.

When you read this line, you wonder how you will use it daily. Imagine this, and you can begin to consider all the possibilities. When you consider all the possibilities, this will provide you with a lot of drive to get started.

Using the effect as if it were a global desire is one approach to boost this significantly. Anything resembling sex, attention from others, greater money, effortless weight loss, or any other effortless reward.

Now, you must begin slowly. You can't call on a stranger's door and claim that purchasing your vacuum cleaner will cause them to have copious amounts of sex with beautiful people as hundreds of dollars fall from the sky.

But, you can gradually relocate them from their current location to the desired one.

This will take careful preparation. For instance, if you sell vacuum cleaners, the end effect of people purchasing your vacuum cleaner will be a cleaner home. A home that is not just cleaner but also cleaner with less effort.

And with less work, they will feel more at ease inviting their friends around, earning them much more respect and admiration.

If you began by claiming that purchasing your vacuum cleaner would garner them a lot of attention and respect from their peers, they would slam the door in your face.

You have something to work with, though; if you establish rapport, find out what's essential to them in keeping a tidy home and progressively elicit how they feel about having guests over.

Simply construct a lengthy chain of cause and effect so they will accept some simple steps between opening the door and purchasing your vacuum cleaner. This can be applied to any product or concept, regardless of size. Simply begin where you are and establish some credible stages leading to your goal.

CHAPTER 11: HELPING OTHERS WITHOUT EXPECTING ANYTHING IN RETURN USING THE POWER OF CAUSE AND EFFECT.

What happens when a fully inflated basketball is dropped on a horizontal, hard surface? Indeed, it does bounce back. What happens when a boomerang is successfully launched through the air without obstructions? True again - it returns.

What happens when you help someone in need without expecting anything in return? As with the ball and the boomerang, it also returns to you. This is valid because of the Law of Cause and Effect, which applies to physical and universal laws.

The Law of Cause and Effect is called the Golden Rule and the Law of the Harvest. You've heard the expressions "Do unto others what you want them to do unto you" and "You reap what you sow." As indicated by the italics in the above sentence, "it" might refer to various objects.

It is possible that we may not know what "it" will be before it returns. Still, we can be certain that whatever "it" is, it is just what we need to aid our personal development or improve our abundance in any situation. It will directly correspond to how we gave. This is a global law or absolute reality. Absolute truth will always be absolute, regardless of human perspectives and conceptions of such constants.

We can't change or modify the truth; it simply exists. Leslie Householder has expressed it: "You can't break a [universal] law; you can only break yourself against it." This principle also pertains to the effectiveness of universal laws.

This principle of Cause and Effect states, "Every effect has a cause, and every cause has an effect. It will work to our advantage if we choose not to violate this law. Nothing ever happens by chance."

We decide of our own free choice to provide aid and assistance in whatever capacity and form we can; by doing so, the "good deed" will also return to us. It may not return in the manner we anticipate, but it will return in due time and of some kind. To what extent do you live by "karma"?

To receive a "result" of equal value, your "cause" must be genuine and selfless. If we seek to aid others for the sole aim of receiving or being perceived as generous by others, then this effect has already happened. For instance, suppose I am a millionaire and conduct a press conference to announce to the world that I am contributing $100,000,000 to aid in treating breast cancer.

What is my reward for doing this?

Wouldn't it be the praise of the entire human race if they knew "how generous" I was?

Most certainly, yeah. I would likely receive worldly recognition and possibly remuneration for my contribution. However, the primary effect of my cause would be the recognition I would receive for such an act.

Let's look at this from a different perspective. Imagine I am in a precarious financial condition and have lost my wife to breast cancer. To prevent others from suffering as I have, I donate the small amount of money left in my bank account to my local breast cancer association, hoping it may be useful in discovering a cure. By law, the prize for my altruistic sacrifice of everything I own will be substantially more than that of the billionaire.

Where is my recompense?

Who knows, but I can be comfortable that it will arrive and will be directly proportional to the degree I am awarded. My "cause," or technique and motivation for giving, is a direct and proportional response to the "result" I will receive.

Does this parable ring a bell?

Have you ever heard of the parable of the widow's mite?

Leslie Householder explains, "Don't perform nice things in the hope that others won't notice and be impressed." As a result, we already "have our recompense."

As we move on with understanding such a potent reality, it is essential to remember that such actions should precede any reward. I believe we should always give before receiving, not the other way around.

We donate because we wish to assist. For a boomerang to "return" to me, I must first "give" it freely so that it might fly its path and return. Such actions necessitate deep confidence in the truth, given that they are required by law, and as such outcomes happen due to our causes, take note of how they came about. Give credit where credit is due, acknowledging that none of this was feasible.

CHAPTER 12: THE LAW OF CAUSE AND EFFECT FOR CORPORATIONS.

The Law of Cause and Effect is also called Karma. That is life's grand "Accounting System." A credit accompanies every debit. Individuals publicly debate this law every day, often about a terrible event. As an example, the bankruptcy of a businessman who amassed his riches by questionable means and ill intentions could be considered by many as a Karmic consequence.

What we don't see as often is the reverse application of the law, such as an inventor who has labored for years to produce a new energy product for the benefit of all people and the environment and then releases his life's work. This individual could become a millionaire during the next many years. This is typically associated with chance rather than The Law of Cause and Effect.

What Ingredients are included?

How can we know with absolute confidence what contributes to the outcome from our vantage point? The more one examines this law, the more it appears to be a combination of acts, intentions, and thoughts. In other words, it would be subject to "Karma" to intentionally inflict injury on someone after methodically preparing for the occurrence.

However, a person who sustains comparable injuries as a passenger in your vehicle and as a result of a total accident is not liable to The Law. The outcome was the same, yet there was no intent or lengthy negative thought preceding the incident.

What is this law's application to business?

In two ways, the Law of Cause and Effect relates to business:

1. The cumulative impact of "Group Karma" on business.

2. The Karma of the enterprise.

Imagine that we are a gangster trying to fill various positions within the group to commit crimes. We will undoubtedly recruit like-minded individuals who can design and execute the group's commercial operations. We can, therefore, confidently assert that the cumulative effect of this group's actions and interactions will affect both the individuals and the group.

Many gang members will come and go throughout time, and the group will continue to operate as usual. Some former members may be in prison, deceased, or have joined other organizations. Our initial gang has moved on to "bigger and better" things.

Anyone with a sincere desire to serve others will be drawn to an organization established to aid homeless individuals. A company will also attract talent that aligns with its activities, prevailing thinking style, and goals. Hence, over time a collective Karma will develop that represents the aggregate of the individuals.

Individuals will benefit from their efforts if this remains the purpose and emphasis of activities. This may emerge as a relaxed, stress-free existence or a profound satisfaction, varying from person to person. For instance, a fresh graduate participating in this activity may be exposed to the appropriate company to launch her career.

What Must Companies Be Aware Of?

Managers within corporations must be highly aware of how the corporation's intentions are communicated to employees and the outside world. For instance, objectives are often described in monetary terms, giving the impression that this is the business's only goal.

Hence, a division of a huge firm may establish a target that reads, "Achieve a minimum profit of $150 million from the growth of new international markets." This is acceptable, and the company should also guarantee that the reasons for its entry into the selected international markets are communicated.

In this instance, the communication of corporate aim may be "To provide stronger and safer building materials at cheaper costs to international markets, where this combination will have a large positive impact on the daily lives of people in the building sector and the general public."

Companies must also be conscious that they have their own Karma based on past actions. The question now is how the organization will respond to the ensuing action when it happens.

A common example would be a pharmaceutical company that released a medicine many years ago with the knowledge that its full effects had not been evaluated or verified. Today, the corporation faces a class action lawsuit from individuals directly or indirectly affected by the product's negative effects.

The corporation must recognize this behavior for what it is and deal with the individuals involved publicly and fairly. This corporation would exacerbate the law's impact by attempting to dodge its duties, even though former employees may have carried out the initial activities.

Last but not least.

There is no better moment to begin educating the employees on The Law of Cause and Effect and its consequences for the company. This approach alone will make people more conscious of their aims, thoughts, and acts and more ready to deal with any challenges resulting from their past intents, ideas, and actions.

Human Resource Departments should investigate the existing information on the topic and plan its incorporation into training and development programs.

The Public Relations personnel must be conscious of communicating the company's internal and external goals. Considering this law, the words used have a much broader scope than was previously believed.

Even the typical political practice of "spin" can have a deliberate ulterior goal to mislead or deceive the populace.

Managers must carefully consider how they communicate the organization's objectives to their employees so that only positive intents that benefit the company, its customers, and the environment are conveyed.

Marketers should be truthful with clients so that no communications are misinterpreted as deceptive or dishonest. Rather than focusing just on the possible rise in revenue, product development personnel should build goods with the end benefits to customers, the environment, and the organization clearly defined.

Like all Natural Laws, this mighty Law will work regardless of our actions. Consequently, we should take the time to comprehend and learn how to live with it.

CHAPTER 13: HAVING BELIEF IN THE LAW OF CAUSE AND EFFECT.

There are Universal Laws, and too often, when trying to materialize, we forget that we are spiritual beings and can't help but manifest what we desire. We look and look, and when we don't see what we planned to manifest, we conclude that our prayer/manifested desire was ineffective.

The first manifestation rule is to have faith. When we violate this rule, we can only manifest what we already believe in. Too often, we feel that negative things will happen if we.

Cause and effect or sacrifice and vibration is the universe's second law.

Energy circulates and moves in circles. So, the more we contribute to the flow of energy by giving, the faster energy will return to us. If we stop the flow, as we do when we stop giving (or, even worse, if we cling too firmly to resources we are not using), the energy flow is stifled. This will block resources from entering our life, regardless of how well we've practiced visualization and manifestation. This is not only good practice; it is a Universal Law.

Provide information to people who require it, and have faith that you will always have access to the information you require. Get rid of the mess in your cellar, and the flow of things will return to your life. If you leave a tip at a restaurant or send a gift to your child or grandchild, tenfold the amount you gave away will come into your life.

In contrast, when you hoard your possessions or keep your wealth out of circulation, you will experience loss apprehension and ultimately see your fortune decline. Fear is one of the lowest frequencies. Once you fall into fear, you can no longer manifest, and you will be caught on a root in the flow of abundance, no longer able to reap what you like from the Creator's cornucopia of riches.

What is Belief?

Does faith imply that you must have faith that you can manifest millions of money tomorrow? Not quite.

Believing is the conviction that the universe will supply what you desire most finely and quickly imaginable.

I've noticed that dealing with dollars is challenging for me. Perhaps it's because I don't have much affection for cash. I've always discovered that abundance comes to me in other forms, whereas for others, dollars come easily.

Nonetheless, I may quickly become enthused about being in a lovely location near the water. Hence, I have often exhibited a waterfront dwelling. Occasionally it is handed to me. That is sometimes made available to me. Occasionally, the rental price is absurdly low and affordable. Recently, a homeowner waited over a year for me to collect the down payment (the home I now own with my partner.)

I could purchase computers and a car for $300 when that was all I could afford. Due to a minor car accident, I have had significant repairs performed on my automobiles and arrived at work on time despite leaving the house rather late.

Quit telling yourself that you can't or won't have _____ until you do _____ or obtain _____ because, as Henry Ford once stated, "whether you believe you can or feel you can't, you will be accurate."

The first guideline of manifestation is to have faith. The second guideline is to quit thinking there won't be enough or that it will be taken away and to exhibit love and faith by maintaining the flow of your energy/wealth/abundance.

We all have habits and vibrations that we can't shake. Many of these radiations and impacts can affect your fate.

When your "free will" is employed appropriately, it enables you to overcome all obstacles that prevent you from expressing your spirit to the utmost extent. Because you are spirit, and you are spirit.

Each human soul will receive a seed of spirit, just as a seed is planted in the land. If you provide the necessary conditions for a seed to grow, it will first emerge from the soil, bloom, and burst into full flower.

The Great Spirit put the seed within each of us; you are our gardener. It is dependent upon your efforts as to whether or not the flower's fullness may be expressed. The Great Spirit can't be expressed through you if you keep the seed in the darkness and don't give it light. Always, you have free will.

When the law is in effect, it is flawless. Always, effect follows cause.

Because you can only reap what you sow, the law of cause and effect is elementary, fundamental, and immutable. No one can modify the chain of cause and effect by a hair's breadth. What is reaped must correspond to what is sown in the soul of each individual.

The effect must follow the cause. In turn, the effect becomes the cause, which sets in motion another effect that produces still another cause. The procedure is continuous.

The law of cause and effect applies to many natural occurrences, regardless of their size, complexity, or simplicity. There is no way to interrupt this sequence.

If cause did not determine the effect, your planet, the universe, and the wide cosmos would be in disarray. The Great Spirit, God the Godhead, and the Ultimate Power would not be the pinnacle of love, knowledge, and perfection if they were not the source of all that exists.

The universe is ruled by divine justice, which has religious and spiritual importance. If it were possible to change the consequences of wrongdoing, this would violate the norms of divine justice, demonstrating that religious and spiritual law is defective and unjust since its pattern can be changed.

Nature must pursue its predetermined course, blind to human will. It has responsibilities and will continue to do so. When people cooperate, they get benefits. Those who labor in harmony with nature can take advantage of the abundance nature has to give.

Whatever good you perform, you benefit from it.

Whatever selfishness you engage in, you will suffer the consequences.

You can't circumvent the laws of nature. You can't express remorse for your actions and simultaneously nullify every consequence resulting from your actions.

CHAPTER 14: LIVING THE LAW OF CAUSE AND EFFECT.

Based on the Law of Cause and Effect, each cause has an effect, and each effect has a cause. Nothing ever happens by chance. Anything you send into the cosmos will return to you.

If you treat others with kindness and respect, they will respond in kind and respect. Never worry about what you will receive; instead, focus on what you can give. When you sow the cause (in this case, compassion and respect for others), the effect will inevitably follow (others treating you with kindness and respect).

Do you require more benevolence in your life? Then sow seeds of kindness wherever you go, and kindness will return to you in abundance.

Do you wish you had more time? Finally, give your time freely through service and volunteering; you will receive another time in return.

Do you require more funds? Then give a tenth of your current wealth to others less fortunate than you, and money will flow back to you!

Do you require improved relationships? Then become a better companion and friend!

Some years ago, I compiled a list of my desired characteristics in my future spouse. After listing all I could think of, I devised a list of 67 attributes I desired in my future husband. I indicated the essential characteristics with an "E" and the non-essential characteristics with a "W." (for wants).

But then I did something extremely essential that I have never heard "experts" discuss when they discuss list-making. As I completed the list, I looked at it and said, "Now I must become this individual." Then I set about becoming the exact individual I had described in my list! I believe this is why it works for some individuals but not others.

There is a significant difference between desiring a million dollars and acquiring one. Wanting is nothing more than idle daydreaming; being needs inspired, continuous effort toward a goal/vision (which, of course, requires the goal/vision, to begin with).

Using my situation as an illustration, there is a significant difference between wanting a wonderful relationship, identifying a great partner, and working to become one yourself!

Because you get back what you sow, plant only quality seeds. Ensure that what you are seeking is not ego-based (wanting more than another person, wanting someone to do something for you, wanting something in return. wanting, wanting, wanting).

Be sure the seeds you plant are deserving of you. You will always reap the benefits if you sow seeds of value and service for others! If you sow the seeds of desire, you will be in a perpetual deficiency situation.

Throughout our lives, we are always acquiring new knowledge, and by the time we reach adulthood, we can rectify many of the mistakes we made as children. We learn from others as we progress, but they are often absent when we seem to need them the most, forcing us to grab the reins and do the best we can with the knowledge we possess.

They say that life is a great teacher, and it is, even though we often get burned or feel bad about the past. Looking back, we see that we fell into many pitfalls not because we did anything bad but because we lacked knowledge. Now that we have learned how to handle the many scenarios we have encountered in the past, we no longer have to deal with these issues or make difficult decisions.

It is useless to cling to the past, as it has passed, and all that was done within it has been our lessons to learn; life is a difficult taskmaster, but I am sure many of us can see others having a more difficult time. Many individuals struggle with their conscience long after events have transpired.

Most people in life don't want to cause harm to anyone or anything, yet they may have sparked chain reactions. When things go out of hand, going other ways and into other people's hands, where they are twisted from the way we intended. Regrettably, our notion becomes so different from what we had originally envisioned.

We are all inventors in one way or another, giving off many things adopted by others, which make them their own while adding their twists to be used for either good or evil. We do not influence another person's mind; consequently, this can and does sometimes backfire, as they say, and we can watch that idea, that act of generosity, heading down a path we did not plan, yet we feel guilty.

Some people in the world assign incorrect tasks to others because they lack the courage to perform them themselves. Thus they put it forth for somebody to execute the deed for them, washing their hands of it, they believe; yet, it is all out in the ether, this of thought and its creativity, and those who emitted the first thought are still neck-deep in it.

We are all accountable for what we have created in this life of the mortal soul, learning and acting based on our views, whether correct or wrong, according to the dictates of our conscience.

CHAPTER 15: HOW TO SURVIVE UNDER A CHALLENGING SITUATION UTILIZING THE LAW OF CAUSE AND EFFECT.

Based on the Law of Cause and Effect, everything you throw into the universe will return to you. Equal and opposite are action and reaction. Focus on what you can give rather than what you can receive.

It happened again. I can't recall what the quarrel was about or its origin, but I recall the effect—anxiety and discomfort that filled my stomach. My first thought was, "Oh no. Not again."

I'm certain you can envision the situation.

Home: a married couple. Disagreement. The ego rears its ugly head. He storms into one room while she sulks into another.

You have the idea.

I entered the kitchen, sat on a stool, and rested my head on the counter. I allowed myself a VERY brief period to let the emotions wash through me because I was so familiar with them. They were quite disagreeable. I let myself one minute to cry before gathering my wits.

I studied the Natural Laws of the Universe or the Rules of Success for many months. I recalled those thoughts generated.

"Thoughts produce" Then, then! I was accountable for this circumstance. Gulp. Possibly, I desired it on some level. (I shuddered at the thought but realized its potential veracity.) My next thought was, "I can learn something from this."

I was not at my most logical, but I did think of a few things.

Was I a serious student initially?

Did I believe these statutes?

This was an ideal opportunity for me to apply the lessons. I considered the "thinking stuff" that Wallace Wattles teaches: There is a thinking stuff from which all things are produced, which, in its original state, permeates, penetrates, and fills the universe's interspaces.

A thought in this substance generates the object envisioned by the concept.

I can make objects in my mind, and by impressing my thoughts upon the formless matter, I can materialize the object I imagine to materialize.

"I MUST CONTEMPLATE."

I was reminded that thankfulness is extremely essential. I felt like Winnie the Pooh when he tapped his finger three times to his temple and said, "Think. Think. Think."

So I expressed gratitude for the experience! It was a difference! I closed my eyes and expressed appreciation for the experience, the pain, and the lessons it had provided. (Thank you for this unpleasant experience.) I then requested assistance.

At that time, I shifted my attention to what I wanted.

I desired to be at ease. I made it up. I believed it.
I desired support during my difficulty. I believed it.
I desired to feel affection for my hubby. I envisioned it by recalling "better times. I then considered it.
I wished for happiness. I imagined it. I believed it.
I desired to gain insight from this event. I allowed myself to be taught the lessons contained within it.
I desired a harmonious relationship. I imagined what that might entail.
I desired for the quarrel to end. I believed it. I let go.
I desired for us to be "fine." I believed it.

And what do you know? WE WERE! I let the experience transpire and LEFT IT BE! I did not dwell on it or any discomfort since I had shifted my perspective and changed what I was "sending to the Universe."

I had a brief period of calm due to applying correct thought processes.

Gotta adore it!

The Law of Cause and Effect teaches us that activity and reaction are of equal magnitude but move in opposite directions. Concentrate on what you can offer rather than what you will receive.

And I would add, observe how rapidly you can change the outcomes by changing your concentration, ideas, and emotions!

CHAPTER 16: CHOOSE A STRONG CAUSE TO APPLY THE LAW OF CAUSE AND EFFECT.

The Law of Cause and Effect is so straightforward that it appears to require no explanation. "A guy will reap what he sows" Galatians 6:7. Regarding growing seeds, I enjoy gardening. My favorite veggie to plant is green beans.

They continue to produce throughout the summer until I am exhausted from harvesting them. As the temperature rises, I am tired of beans and neglect to water their plants, resulting in their demise. When I am hungry for green beans again, I must open a can and remember how much tastier the beans from the garden were.

Opening a can may be simpler, but the experience is not as gratifying.

What type of fulfillment do you seek in life?

What desires do you have?

Perhaps they consist of more money, better relationships with friends and family, better health, a better job, better education, and more enjoyment. How can you select a cause for each one to obtain what you desire?

I propose that focusing your attention on a compelling cause will have various beneficial impacts. Let me give you an example. I sought a significant cause to animate my mission statement and assist me in becoming the wonderful person I know I am. I said, "I will provide exceptional service in every aspect of my life."

My neighbor placed a sign for sale in her yard. I was annoyed despite having no control over the situation. I did not want anyone to disturb my tranquil situation. As a result of my recent nasty thoughts about her, the energy between us was not as pleasant as it once was, and that was my fault. I determined it was time to change both my thinking and actions.

Sunday was her birthday, which I learned from the church bulletin. I might have wished her a "Happy Birthday" during church, but I wished to do something special. The desire itself began to lighten my heart and bring a smile to my face.

I contemplated at home what I could gift her that she would appreciate. I chose a freshly acquired CD that I knew she would adore. I wrapped it and retrieved a card from my box. I wrote a real and personal note to her and went next door. She welcomed me into her home, and we had a fantastic twenty-minute conversation.

She stated that the card was her favorite part of the Album. We embraced and exchanged "I love you"s. I departed with a smile and a spring in my stride and thought I might have simply wished someone "Happy Birthday" in church!

This is a basic example, but when I consider "extraordinary service," it is simpler to raise my thoughts to a higher level and provide my best in any situation. Instead of simply inquiring about a person's well-being, I may concentrate and actively listen.

Instead of generating a list of tasks, I might determine what is most important and concentrate on its accomplishment. Instead of eating whatever is available, I can consume nutritious foods and exercise. Instead of performing well, I have the option of doing better. Instead of being superior, I can be exceptional.

Knowing and consciously applying the Law of Cause and Effect has given me faith in the law. That applies to goods money can buy and those it can't. Instead of being content with the status quo, I might take extraordinary measures to advance my business.

Instead of expecting my students to achieve average outcomes, I may encourage them to strive for excellence and accomplish extraordinary feats. Since I am sowing these seeds, I anticipate a bountiful and joyful harvest in all aspects of my life. How does your garden grow? It is your decision. That's the law!

CHAPTER 17: DON'T REMAIN CONFINED TO THE CHAINS OF CAUSE AND EFFECT.

The universal Law of Cause and Effect is the most fundamental of laws. The law demonstrates that every action of a person has repercussions. You will receive good deeds if you perform good acts.

Whatever you deposit into the vast bank of the cosmos is what you will receive back. If you harm others, you will suffer injury in the future. Some say, "Look at this person; he's a thief who never gets punished for his acts." That is not the case. We invented time to measure things that can't be measured.

Occasionally, we watch individuals suffering while those who cause their agony appear to live happily ever after. Don't misunderstand; these individuals will eventually pay for the consequences of their actions.

Because time is an illusion, we don't see the significance of the Law of Cause and Effect or the Law of Karma.

One might inquire, "What does this law have to do with prosperity?" "Everything." Sometimes, we prevent wonderful things from entering our lives due to our past actions. You can make this law work for you if you are aware of the positive and negative actions you have taken.

Give the positive ones to the cosmos and make amends for the negative ones. Provide the afflicted individual with a solution to a scenario in which you were involved. If that person is no longer in our lives, we should try to do something good for another person and offer this action to the universe as compensation for our former error.

Once we accomplish this, we facilitate the flow of divine energy throughout the universe via our bodies. Once we recognize our mistakes, forgiving is essential to implement the law of forgiveness. We forgive ourselves for the mistakes we have made in the past and others for the wrongs they have committed against us. Whom do we pardon?

We allow divine energy to flow all around us with this action. Some believe that by taking this action, you are helping others, whereas everything you do is for your mental health and benefit. Occasionally, we argue for four or five days after the other party has already forgotten everything.

When we harbor resentment for someone, we restrict our energy and circulate the Law of Cause and Effect against ourselves by emitting negativity into the universe. Everything we put into life, we will receive back.

When you wish to attract material or spiritual goods, you must first visualize them in your mind before they can manifest. You can't bring anything into this dimension if you are unsure about your desires. Deciding what you desire and visualizing it activates the creative law of prosperity.

Our brain is a universe-perfect computer. It enables us to plan and realize our dreams. Scientists who have studied the brain are astonished by the inability of some hypnotized individuals to distinguish between reality and what they believe to be reality.

The subconscious mind operates peculiarly; for the mind, there is no difference between imagining a new car and having one. If you place a chilly coin in a person's hand under a hypnotic trance and tell them that it is extremely hot, they will believe it is hot. Even if the coin is cold, the guy will burn his hand when it fell to the ground.

Watch the lives and deaths of tyrants and other individuals who caused enormous suffering to humanity throughout history. Some people disregard this commandment because it is tough to live a life of integrity when it is difficult, but it is easier to be a crook and face the price. I know a priest who, whenever he was leaving a location, would say to his friends,

"Be good." I asked him, "Why do you always use the same phrase?" He stated, "I am reminding myself to be nice as I remind others of our agreement with God, which is good to us 24 hours a day, seven days a week."

Unless you are a saint, being completely good is nearly always difficult. Once you begin maturing, you tend to perform admirably whenever possible. Growth is a process that requires a lifetime. Consequently, it is advisable to start as early as feasible.

Be careful what you think most of the time since you will become the product of your thoughts. As we begin fantasizing, our subconscious mind will follow us and attempt to instruct our conscious mind on making our fantasies a reality. Once, it was stated, "Our thoughts are prayers." Whatever we think about becomes an invitation for it to enter our lives.

CONCLUSION.

The Law of Cause and Effect has scientific and metaphysical foundations. Early in childhood, we all naturally understand the relationship between Cause and Effect on a subconscious level. When we began to weep, and our mother brought us a warm milk bottle, we saw that sobbing in such a manner typically yielded the desired result.

Causality refers to the direct relationship between causes and effects. This establishes a causal relationship between one action and another event, whether by physical or non-physical methods.

This law doesn't observe evaluating judgment; it is merely a driving force. A piece of metal fell from an airplane and struck your friend in the head as he walked to the party store on the corner, instantly killing him. You are upset, but what, if anything, would you blame?

Would you blame the plane or gravity?

Could you fault your friend's timing for leaving the house precisely when the piece of metal struck him?

Cause and Effect don't assign blame, nor is it beneficial to assign blame. The Law of Cause and Effect is an element of life that happens continuously and independently of our comprehension, yet it is a principle that we apply constantly.

Maple trees disperse their seeds, which germinate and produce further maple trees. Storm clouds gather, then precipitation begins to fall. The earth's single revolution causes the day to turn into night. The wind is accelerating the movement of the clouds. These are all Cause and Effect events that we did not cause.

The Law of Cause and Effect does teach us essential lessons. Through direct experience and emulation, we can perceive certain causes as consequences we desire or seek to avoid.

If you observe people getting intoxicated and always having awful hangovers, you can not want to personalize the experience. You gained second-hand knowledge of what they endured. The booze was the cause, and the following morning's hangover was the effect.

Sometimes we can't learn from examples and must experience Cause and Effect. Ultimately, when these individuals become intoxicated, they appear to be having a wonderful time. Thus you become intoxicated and have a hangover. What did you anticipate?

Often, direct experience is required to understand the link between Cause and Effect. The recurrence of this law teaches us what we need to know on occasion.

Mathematics might be able to explain the Law of Cause and Effect but not necessarily why. Metaphysics recognizes that there is a scientific formula for this principle and can do so without comprehending the formula. Interestingly, metaphysical ideas interpret the Law of Cause and Effect as a mental and universally conscious force, which helps explain this law's effect on us.

In metaphysical circles and certain Eastern faiths, the principle of the Law of Attraction governs the Law of Cause and Effect. The connections between these two laws are well-established and can't be disentangled.

If you consistently inflict agony on others and experience pain, you have no one else to blame. The cause is the suffering you caused, and the effect is the suffering you endured. In the Law of Attraction, cause and effect are manifested extremely naturally. This law states that we receive what we send forth.

Giving out nice acts results in positive manifestations returning to you. At any one time, you are complete, 100 percent subject to the effects of the environment. No matter what happens, you will respond appropriately. Simultaneously, the universe around you is entire, one hundred percent subject to your influence. Regardless of your actions or inactions, the world will react to you. Hence, you are the cause.

You are simultaneous "the cause" and "at the effect." You are both the victim and the maker of your life. Both are true. However, at any given time, you can only experience yourself as one or the other.

When you feel you are at the effect, you are powerless. Instead of controlling your circumstances, they are in control of you. You are victimized. You lose your confidence, your energy, and your efficacy.

You are at the effect whenever you are upset or in an area of your life that is not functioning. Observe how agonizing this is. Find a time when you were experiencing the effects of something and decided you had had enough. You then took your situation by the horns and began dealing with it.

Consider how you felt at the time. Instantaneously, you regained your power. Instead of your circumstances being on top of you, you have risen above them. You became assured and full of vitality. Without your knowledge, you shifted from the effect to the cause.

You can plan your course when you live your life at the cause. You can have your fantasies come true. When you dwell on the effect, you can only generate greater agony. The opportunity of life is to learn to live your life at cause. To accomplish this, you must avoid remaining at the effect.

By denying the truth about something, you put yourself in jeopardy. A circumstance is present in your life, and you are struggling against it. When you do this, you give your power to whatever you resist. You become the victim and the effect of your actions.

To regain your authority, submit to the reality of the situation. Determine what action you need to take based on the facts of the way your circumstance is. Then, perform that action. As soon as you achieve this, you move from being the effect to the cause.

This book is part of an ongoing collection called "Laws of the Universe"

- ➢ Laws of Assumption.
- ➢ Law of Vibration
- ➢ Law of Polarity
- ➢ Law of Cause & Effect
- ➢ Law of Compensation
- ➢ Law of Correspondence
- ➢ Law of Divine Oneness
- ➢ Law of Rhythm
- ➢ Law of Relativity
- ➢ Law of Perpetual Transmutation of Energy
- ➢ Law of Inspired
- ➢ Law og Gravity
- ➢ Law of Gender
- ➢ Law of Gestation
- ➢ Law of Reciprocity
- ➢ Law of Purpose
- ➢ Law of Infinite Possibility
- ➢ Law of Unwavering Faith
- ➢ Law of Constant Motion
- ➢ Law of Free Will
- ➢ Law of Expectation/Expectancy
- ➢ Law of Attraction.

Other Series by Sherry Lee

"Spiritual Attraction."

- Ask Believe Receive.
- Faith Like a Mustard Seed.
- You Were Made for Such a Time as This.
- Let Go and Just Let God Handle it for You.
- You Have Not Because You Ask Not.
- Not my Will Lord but Let Your Will be Done.
- Asking for This or Something Better.
- What is your Why.
- God said 365 Times in the Bible; DO NOT BE AFRAID.
- 10, 100, and 1,000 Fold Increase.
- Immeasurable More than I Can Hope or Imagine.
- All Things are Possible, If you Believe.

"Opening and Balancing Your Chakra's"

- Unblocking your 3rd Eye
- Opening and Balancing your Heart Chakra
- Opening and Balancing your Crown Chakra
- Opening and Balancing your Throat Chakra
- Opening and Balancing your Solar Plexu Chakra

- Opening and Balancing your Sacral Chakra
- Opening and Balancing your Root Chakra.

"Why Alternative Medicine Works"

- Why Yoga Works
- Why Chakra Works
- Why Massage Therapy Works
- Why Reflexology Works
- Why Acupuncture Works
- Why Reiki Works
- Why Meditation Works
- Why Hypnosis Works
- Why Colon Cleansing Works
- Why NLP (Neuro Linguistic Programming) Works
- Why Energy Healing Works
- Why Foot Detoxing Works
- Why Singing Bowls Works.
- Why Tapping Works
- Why Muscle Testing Works.

"Using Sage and Smudging"

- Learning About Sage and Smudging

- Sage and Smudging for Love
- Sage and Smudging for Health and Healing
- Sage and Smudging for Wealth and Abundance
- Sage and Smudging for Spiritual Cleansing
- Sage and Smudging for Negativity.

"Learning About Crystals"

- Crystals for Love
- Crystals for Health
- Crystals for Wealth
- Crystals for Spiritual Cleansing
- Crystals for Removing Negativity.

"What Every Newlywed Should Know and Discuss Before Marriage."

- Newlywed Communication on Money
- Newlywed Communication on In-laws
- Newlywed Communication about Children.
- Newlywed Communication on Religion.
- Newlywed Communication on Friends.
- Newlywed Communication on Retirement.
- Newlywed Communication on Sex.
- Newlywed Communication on Boundaries.

- Newlywed Communication on Roles and Responsibilities.

"Health is Wealth."

- Health is Wealth
- Positivity is Wealth
- Emotions is Wealth.
- Social Health is Wealth.
- Happiness is Wealth.
- Fitness is Wealth.
- Meditating is Wealth.
- Communication is Wealth.
- Mental Health is Wealth.
- Gratitude is Wealth.

"Personal Development Collection."

- Manifesting for Beginners
- Crystals for Beginners
- How to Manifest More Money into your Life.
- How to work from home more effectively.
- How to Accomplish more in Less Time.
- How to End Procrastination.
- Learning to Praise and acknowledge your Accomplishments.
- How to Become your Own Driving Force.

- Creating a Confident Persona.
- How to Meditate.
- How to Set Affirmations.
- How to Set and Achieve your Goals.
- Achieving Your Fitness Goals.
- Achieving Your Weight Loss Goals.
- How to Create an Effective Vision Board.

Other Books By Sherry Lee:

- Repeating Angel Numbers
- Most Popular Archangels.

Author Bio

Sherry Lee. Sherry enjoys reading personal development books, so she decided to write about something she is passionate about. More books will come in this collection, so follow her on Amazon for more books.

Thank you for your purchase of this book.

I honestly do appreciate it and appreciate you, my excellent customer.

God Bless You.

Sherry Lee.

Printed in Great Britain
by Amazon